Poetic Release

From Negative Thinking

A POETRY
COLLECTION OF
HEALING WORDS

Copyright © 2022 by Angela De Palma

All rights reserved. No part of this publication may be reproduced, distributed, or transmitted in any form by any means, including photocopying, recording, or other electronic methods without the prior written permission of the author, except in the case of brief quotations embodied in reviews and certain other noncommercial uses permitted by copyright law. For permission requests, please contact the author.

First printed in 2022
Printed on demand in United States, Australia and United Kingdom.

Edited by Laura Field
Cover & Interior by Turtle Publishing

Published by Turtle Publishing

Dedicated to Kevin Bursnall my rock, Laura Field my editor who has helped build my confidence and skill as a poet and Shannon Stone my best friend in business who has supported me faithfully since we became friends.

Also dedicated to my Mum and Dad, Michela and Claudio who gifted me my precious life.

Contents

Barren is the landscape	1
The path back to purpose	2
Time	3
Ten minutes	4
Breathe deep	5
Release from worry	6
Falling behind	7
Release from self-beration	8
To spiral down is optional	9
Diverting from the habitual pathway	10
First blood	11
The gift	13
Death bed companion	14
The aftermath of my Mum's passing	15
Grateful for the mundane	16
Bonds of family	17

Healing a rift	18
Compassion	19
Winning the game of uncertainty	20
Weathered by time	21
Authenticity	22
Freedom from should	23
Grounded in action	24
A space of calm	25
Contentment	26
I remember	27
Self investment	28
Recommitting to different thought patterns	29
My witness	30
The lies are getting more unbelievable	31
Uncertainty	32
Renewal	33
Rhythm of humanity	34
About the Author	35

A collection of poems exploring release from negative thought patterns.

This collection of poems reflects my journey of understanding and healing and is dedicated to everyone who struggles with self-doubt and self-criticism. Writing is my way of exploring and releasing old patterns and limitations.

As a professional coach, I have learned that this struggle is real for many of us. You will find pathways that work by reaching out for support, therapy, and coaching. Invest in yourself and never give up.

I hope these poems inspire you to find your own release from the damaging impact of a tyrannical inner critic.

For more information and support, please visit my websites. I would love to have you join the community and learn about the services on offer.

www.angeladepalma.com
www.shesimplyimpacts.com
www.visionaccountable.com.au

Barren is the landscape

Barren is the landscape,
Miles and miles of flat.
The holding of nothing.
In the nothingness, pure possibility
may still exist
If the mind is willing to yield
It's rigidity.
The dry cracks of earth widen
As thoughts decipher a new paradigm.

The path back to purpose

The path back to purpose
Is the company I keep in solitude.
A tea party of one.
Home within my mind
To create.
Dreams
Fashioned into form.
Action emerges.

Time

I value my time.

Governed by choice.
Bright and focused.
Worth more than the price of gold itself.

It is finite.
Protected with boundaries.
Guards my vision, goals and legacy.
Engaging foresight to make best use of it!!
Priorities -

Prioritize.

Ten minutes

Ten minutes.
What can happen in ten minutes?
A finite drop of time -
A drop of rain remaining as the sun emerges -
The sky purges and in ten minutes the
landscape is altered.
Transformation:
The elation that ten minutes of brief focus
Can unleash.
A sense of purpose.
Relief.
Ten minutes each day,
To notice
could align your life.
Each ten minute bite
Just might,
Be all it takes.

Breathe deep

Forgot to breathe
Flight fear.
Grasp at air.
Lungs fill-
A forest of calm unlocks with each deep breath.
The cool air
Restores health.
The moment is sweetened.
Perspectives widen.
Fresh evidence that providence is one deep breath away.

Release from worry

Twisted up in knots
It's all made up, worry.
The mind quickly conjures,
Never stops to ponder-
Is this helpful?
It simply regurgitates
The image,
One thought crowding another.
In our waking slumber
We fall prey
Receiving
Believing
Quick to suffer.
Buffer, rather;
Engage your filters
Use your wits
Keep what's useful
Discard the rest.
Rest
And remain in peace.

Falling behind

Behind is a construct.
Living in the future.
Stress blinds vision.
Resulting in self judgment.
Let go.

Flux and flow,
Allowing perspective.
Come back to now.
What is the focus?
Align my mind to the present.
Immersion.

Release from self-beration

Brutal Beater has come to tea
Unannounced.
She takes a seat
Settles in.
What are you here to talk about?
How bad I am?
What a terrible job I'm doing?
I know her game.
And as we talk, I pour her tea.
Unbeknownst to Brutal
Hers is poisoned peppermint
And as she sips, she shrinks with pain
And I regain my calm,
Released from self-beration.

To spiral down is optional

Feeling like shit
but still smelling fragrant.
The glass is half empty.
The glass is half full.
Life is abundant, teeming with security,
prosperity.
My mind wants to return to familiar
negativity.
The choice is mine,
to feel divine,
or not.

No circumstances are perfect.
Vulnerability exists on the edge.
The fringe where two states collide.
To rise takes effort, intention.
Which thought lives in truth?
To spiral down is optional
I aim for the baseline of the neutral zone.

Diverting from the habitual pathway

Brutal beater dropped by again:
The door was open.
She was on a rampage with a stick.
She said I keep repeating the same mistakes
and she's sick of me.
I was caught off guard and took a beating.
I'm black and blue, bruises meeting.
Crying.
Lying helpless.
Out of control: How to diffuse?
Forgive
Deserve,
despite my imperfections.
Next time, I'll be more wary.
Barring the way.
Diverting the habitual neural pathway.

First blood

First blood.
Silent whispers,
A thud of shame.
Ashamed of what?
What have I done?
Must be guilty,
Filthy,
Must be disgusting,
Worthy only of rejection.

Inferior status.
Handed down from one generation to the next.
Ashamed of the feminine.
The misogyny programmed.
She embodied it,
Lived it
And passed it down.
The low self esteem.
No kind embrace,
Or kind words.
Be free of shame

Strong in the feminine.

Understand the impact,
Generations of oppression.

Psychological isolation
Gives birth to determination
To break the cycle of disempowerment.

The gift

In the narcissist's grip.
You don't realize-
Quick to be discarded.
It is not a question of loyalty.
You don't cooperate, toe the line,
The vine is cut.
And you drop.
Stopped in your tracks.
Left writhing in pain.
Emotionally abandoned.
A conditional love.
A cold calculated transaction,
Fabricated in the self-serving mind.
The blame is not yours.
The flip side is,
It sets you free.
When you finish grieving,
You rebuild yourself.
Take ownership.
Rejection becomes the source of
empowerment.

Death bed companion

Death bed companion
The phone call
The inevitable
She's going
Come now
Jump on a plane
Relieved
At home
Straight by her side
Family gathered
Life coming to pass
Identity unraveled by a decade of dementia
Body in shut down
Over a three night vigil
Moment by moment
Calmly waiting
Last breath looming
Grateful to share the final moments of Mum's life

The aftermath of my Mum's passing

My mum died.
I'm left
Still alive,
Walking this earth without her.
The cord cut.
I'm floating in grief,
Reorganizing my beliefs
about life
priorities
time.
I'm a mess, dressed in resilience.
Feeling terrible and relieved.
Witnessing her suffering was insufferable.
Suffocating my delusions about dying.
I'm crying on the inside.
The roller coaster of grief
Continues to rise and fall.
I accept my vulnerability is inescapable.
I grasp for the mundane.

Grateful for the mundane

To end and begin with awareness
The mundane is a privileged game
Appreciation is an attitude to cultivate
Same pattern moment by moment
Breathing in,
Breathing out.
Silently working in life giving order,
Without it
The human organism collapses,
Wilts and withers.
The mundane slips through our grip.
Reality suddenly trips and churns.
Survival kicks in.
And the road to regain the mundane
Begins all over again.

Bonds of family

Beginning anew with old relationships.
Giving the benefit of the doubt.
Sprouting new love neurons.
Letting go of old thoughts,
blame, hurt.
Bonds of family run deep.
The first encounter with belonging.
Years of disconnection, disintegration on the verge
of annihilation.
The bond is strained,
not broken.
The chosen pathway is
Forgiving
Flicking the switch, activate the current
Which lay dormant like seeds in winter.

Healing a rift

Friendship cracked by hurt and
misunderstandings,
Masked by layers of pretense.
Difficult conversations require truthful words,
Courage to voice the avoided,
Space for honesty to speak.

You could cut the tension.
The awkwardness becomes impossible:
I risk and lay all bare.
The words shine light on perceived offenses
And responsibility is recognised.
Remorse sets in -
Tears flow -
Love emerges:

We travel together to the other side.
The joy of connection is restored.

Compassion

Every drop of compassion
For self and others
Yields gallons of blessings.
When pressed with a choice
Dissolve discontent,
Entitlement.

Expecting happiness and harmony on a silver platter,
It is not a matter to take for granted.

As we rent space on this earth,
It is easy to forget
Compassion gives back
When we least expect it.

Winning the game of uncertainty

Can I trust myself to stay?
Can I commit and weather the storms?
The uncertainty.
Generate my ultimate reality
Fatality.
Years of running have taken a toll
But not stripped me.
My ability to orchestrate is still intact -
Peel back the deep layers,
Penetrate,
Face the insecurity.
Lessons learned are my life long companions.
Despite feeling vulnerable
I keep trying,
Betting on instinct,
Giving it all I've got:
I'm winning.

Weathered by time

Weathered by time
But not withered within.
Dedication to healing,
the aging process reverses.
Internal organs rejoice,
DNA mutates.
My body scrubbed and peeled,
Dead skin exfoliating,
My fate is not sealed.
Exuberance regenerates -
Vitality penetrates -
The mind is calm,
Battle scars disarmed.
I am at peace.

Authenticity

Authenticity is simple yet hard.
Fear
Of revealing,
Being found out.

Being human.
Unique.
A perfect imperfect.
Comparing myself to others
Wreaks havoc on my happiness.
Harsh self-judgement,
Destroys my vitality.
Not good enough,
suppresses action,
Creativity.

Despite this habit,
Living truthfully
Is still a possibility.
Within our control.

Have courage.
It's your authentic vulnerability,
That is interesting.

Freedom from should

A should is a should
And a will is a will
I will. I do.
I commit.
I no longer sit and contemplate.
I go all in.
I change my behavior
I train my brain
New neuro pathways form
I'm a "should" reformed and transformed.

Grounded in action

It's all afoot
Materialized through action.
Action is my religion:
I do, I play, I laugh, I sing
I bring my vision to life,
One small step at a time.

One step leads to another.

And as the thought forms
Through each and every tiny step,
Confidence builds
And enthusiasm slowly grows.
Emerging reality confirms possibility.

Vision and practicality merge,
Transformed into bite-sized-pieces of doing.

The future has now become the now.

A space of calm

A state of balance.
Acceptance.
I am only stressed if I undress the present,
and expose the moment to anxiety.
Remaining clothed
Needing to regulate.
The breath keeps me in check,
a space of calm.

Contentment

Feeling pleased.
Frequented by contentment -
The work pays off:
The meditating, the coaching,
The endeavor to achieve.
Smelling the roses, the perfume is sweet
It's a treat to be alive.
It does not happen by chance,
Rather by effort and focus.
Conscious of peril and pitfalls,
Years of trial and error,
Weathering the storms and the mistakes.
Restocking provisions of sustenance,
Engaging the Sherpas,
Staying on track,
Committing,
Dedicating to the vision.
True contentment
Becomes my new frequency.

I remember

I remember,
But sometimes it is better to forget,
Lest the memories infect my present focus.
My mental rehearsal
Of what I'm creating -
Gestating
Feelings of future elation,
The celebration of immeasurable gratitude.

Self investment

I invest in myself.
I plant the seeds that will yield my happiness.
It's not a question of luxury,
It's a matter of necessity.
I am still vulnerable,
Falling prey to the belief that creating the life of my dreams
Was never possible and never will be.
Who am I to invest in myself?
Who am I?
I'm on shaky ground, but profoundly solid in my commitment.
I reach out for support, contorting my old conditioning.
I'm living proof it's possible -
I'm doing it.

Recommitting to different thought patterns

Feeling on the top of the world
Productive, abundant, hopeful.
Boom.

Confidence plummet.
It can strike at any time
One trigger can cause a drop
Stop me in my tracks.
Send me spiraling,
Down the cavern
Dark and cold,
Sinking and shivering.
Lurking saboteurs,
Brutal beater and her friends,
Smug in their dark victory.
The stories they spin,
seem so real.

I will choose my reality.
Recommitting to different thought patterns.
Taking me higher.
Regaining hard won equilibrium
Mastery returns.

My witness

My witness
Who is she,
That sits over me?
Observing my actions and reactions
with curiosity.
My negative impulses.

Objective and detached,
Providing perspective,
She studies my pulse,
Guides my insight.
She is part of me.

I pause.

Choose her wisdom
For my counsel.

The lies are getting more unbelievable

My witness
Flicked the switch,

Caught a glimpse,
And in the glare,
The ambushers took flight.
Brutal and her friends loathe light.
Disarmed, yet again!
Nice try.
The lies are getting more unbelievable.
Easily recognisable.

Uncertainty

There is more,
I just don't know what there is yet.
I simply know that I must continue.
Must have faith.

Life is not a race.
It's an expression and a reaction.

Revealing the layers takes time.
There is no beginning, middle or end.
There is only now.
The now is where we live.
To not know is a truth.
Transforming uncertainty into trust.

Breathe in,
Breathe out.
Focus on breath.
Still safe.
Momentarily calm.
Still uncertain?
This imperfect moment is our perfection.

Renewal

I'm in the forest,
but I'm not lost.
I'm listening.
Receiving.
And as I look up at the tallest tree,
And down at the deep wide roots embedded,
I'm fed oxygen and life force.
Earth holds me.
I reflect and acknowledge.
Speak. Release.
Nature's influence,
The source of all life,
Renews me.

Rhythm of humanity

The beat lives in the heart,
The beat lives in the street.
Rhythm of humanity,
Interconnecting,
Breathes through body,
Breezy and easy,
In and out.
Connect back to breath,
Worthy and deserving,
Effortless pulsating.

About the Author

For two plus decades Angela has worked as an entrepreneur and more recently as a business accountability, career, personal branding coach and consultant. She works with entrepreneurs and professionals helping them simplify complexity and transform confusion, doubt, overwhelm and bottlenecks. The results are smart personal branding, business and career strategies unleashing passion, leverage, and action. Her questioning and auditing skills have a knack for extracting relevant information into step by step action plans.

She helps clients see what they don't see in themselves or their business, and motivates them to clarify their vision and turn their goals into reality. A big part of her work is helping clients overcome mind-set obstacles to advancing their career and life.

www.ingramcontent.com/pod-product-compliance
Lightning Source LLC
Chambersburg PA
CBHW020331010526
44107CB00054B/2074

9780645395488